SINÉAD MORRISSEY was born in Portadown and ⬚⬚⬚
Dublin. She received the Patrick Kavanagh Aw⬚⬚⬚
an Eric Gregory Award in 1996, and the Rupe⬚⬚ ⬚⬚
Award in 2002. In the same year she was awarded a MacCauley
Fellowship from the Irish Arts Council, was Writer-in-Residence at the
Royal Festival Hall for the Poetry International Festival, and was short-
listed for the T.S. Eliot Prize for her second collection, *Between Here and
There.* She became Writer-in-Residence at the Seamus Heaney Centre
for ⬚⬚ try, Queen's University, Belfast, in 2002.

Also by Sinéad Morrissey from Carcanet

There Was Fire in Vancouver
Between Here and There

SINÉAD MORRISSEY

The State of the Prisons

CARCANET

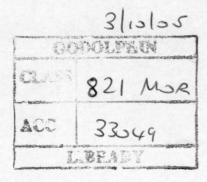
First published in Great Britain in 2005 by
Carcanet Press Limited
Alliance House
Cross Street
Manchester M2 7AQ

A CIP catalogue record for this book is available from the British Library
ISBN 1 85754 775 6
The publisher acknowledges financial assistance from Arts Council England

Typeset by XL Publishing Services, Tiverton
Printed and bound in England by SRP Ltd, Exeter

for Jean Bleakney

Acknowledgements

Acknowledgements are due to the following magazines and anthologies where some of these poems have previously appeared: *Agenda*, *Being Alive* (Bloodaxe, 2004), *Bloomsday Magazine*, *Cuírt*, *Dancing With Kitty Stobling* (Lilliput, 2004), *Fortnight*, *Metre*, *P.E.N. International Magazine*, *PN Review*, *Poetry Daily* (www.poetrydaily.com), *Poetry Ireland Review*, *Poetry London*, *Poetry Wales*, *The New Irish Poets* (Bloodaxe, 2004), *The Stinging Fly*, *The Wake Forest Series of Irish Poetry 1* (Wake Forest University Press, 2004), and *Writers' Train* (British Council, 2004).

'The Second Lesson of the Anatomists' and 'The Wound Man' were both commissioned by Ruth Borthwick of the Royal Festival Hall as part of Poetry International 2002. 'In Praise of Salt' was commissioned by Radio 4 and broadcast on National Poetry Day 2002. 'China' was commissioned by the British Council in 2004.

Thanks to the British Council for a seat on the Writers' Train across China (2003), and for trips to Malta (2003), Cyprus (2004) and Hungary (2004).

Thanks to the staff and trustees of Hawthornden Castle for a fellowship in February 2002, where the poem 'The State of the Prisons' was researched and composed.

Grateful thanks to the Seamus Heaney Centre for Poetry at Queen's University, Belfast, and to the Arts Council of Northern Ireland, for a generous three-year residency.

Contents

Flight 9
The Second Lesson of the Anatomists 11
Forty Lengths 12
Genetics 13
Pilots 14
Lullaby 16
Contrail 17
Little House in the Big Woods 18
Juist 20
China 22
The Gobi from Air 31
Polar 32
On Omitting the Word 'Just' from my Vocabulary 33
Advice 34
Reading the Greats 35
In Praise of Salt 36
The Wound Man 37
Clocks 38
Aunt Sarah's Cupboards and Drawers 39
Absences Also 40
Icarus 41
Forgiveness 42
Driving Alone on a Snowy Evening 43
Migraine 44
The Yellow Emperor's Classic 46
Zero 48
Stepfather 49
The State of the Prisons 51

Notes 60

Flight

There he saw one Anne Bridlestone *drove through the streets by an officer of the same corporation, holding a rope in his hand, the other end fastened to an engine called the branks, which is like a crown, being of iron with a great gag or tongue of iron; and that is the punishment which magistrates do inflict upon chiding and scolding women; and he hath often seen the like done to others.*

England's Grievance Discovered (1655)

After the murder of our blessèd Martyr,
After the slaughter of the rout at Worcester,
His son the rightful king went into hiding –
Here as a woodcutter, there as a serving-man –
Disguising the telltale milk-white of His skin
By the dye of rotted walnuts. 1651:
The Year of Our Lord that my husband bridled me
And I have learned to hold my tongue in company.

*

He could not remain unrecognised for long,
Majesty being so natural unto Him,
It soon shone forth. But was He loved!
He walked upon the bones of England,
Sought solace at farms and hid in the crowns of trees
And all of nature shadowed Him. His enemies
Sifted the land and still His face was not revealed.
It is my love of Him bleeds when I speak out loud.

*

He has stood in a fall of rain
While Cromwell's men sang psalms against Him
And did not venture in. He has seen women
Sink to their knees and then raise their hand in blessing.
My husband desires a sign.
But for all his reading of *Revelation*
I say heaven admits its own
And it is Him. The jaw-straps tighten.

The changeling Prince vanished to France.
Deadwinter dismembers us. Christmas consumes its own bright fire
And blazes by its absence. There is too much law
To live by, and I have torn my face
In two by swallowing silence.
My husband leads me through the marketplace
As the village women gape.

The Second Lesson of the Anatomists

See how the inside belies our skin,
say the anatomists,
after showing us how freakishly we split;

the outside smooth and assiduous
unto itself, while the inside
baffles and seethes...

The lung-wonder held over the heart-wonder
and the heart-wonder bleeding, emptying, re-bleeding,
and spit, in different colours, oiling their hands.

Are all skins as effortlessly deceptive as this?
The thin film over the ocean? Doors?
Or this evening, for instance,

in which darkness and a river
play both mother and father
in supporting a glass room?

There is a party going on. There is wine
and a light fixture being obedient
unto itself. And then there is this spillage

in the centre
from somewhere stranger and more extravagant
which has drawn us all here.

I think of the second lesson of the anatomists.
I think of eggshells cracking open
from the inside.

For we have hallways to discover in one another like nerves.
And childhoods, and love affairs, and drownings, and faithfulness
by which language has occurred.

Forty Lengths

Before goggles, the pool was a catch of beleaguered heads
being raced against each other by omnipotence.

But now that I, too, have been strapped back and capped
like a pre-war flying enthusiast –

shoulders to the rear, the aerodynamic necessity
of not having hair – I see

how solidly we occur under water.
Now all the world's a blur, except for down here

in this makeshift polar enclosure
where I follow one white-limbed swimmer after another

to the wall. We do not resembles fishes, so much as frogs
or the diving waterboatman with his fringed hind legs.

And I find myself back – to the womb,
most obviously, but even better than that – to the film

I played in my head as a child
to make myself sleep: me up in the sky

like Lucy, not needing to breathe, or be tired, or be told, or be older –
wishboning through the stratosphere.

Genetics

My father's in my fingers, but my mother's in my palms.
I lift them up and look at them with pleasure –
I know my parents made me by my hands.

They may have been repelled to separate lands,
to separate hemispheres, may sleep with other lovers,
but in me they touch where fingers link to palms.

With nothing left of their togetherness but friends
who quarry for their image by a river,
at least I know their marriage by my hands.

I shape a chapel where a steeple stands.
And when I turn it over,
my father's by my fingers, my mother's by my palms

demure before a priest reciting psalms.
My body is their marriage register.
I re-enact their wedding with my hands.

So take me with you, take up the skin's demands
for mirroring in bodies of the future.
I'll bequeath my fingers, if you bequeath your palms.
We know our parents make us by our hands.

Pilots

It was black as the slick-stunned coast of Kuwait
over Belfast Lough when the whales came up
(bar the eyelights of aeroplanes, angling in into the airport
out of the east, like Venus on a kitestring being reeled
to earth). All night they surfaced and swam
among the detritus of Sellafield and the panic
of godwits and redshanks.

                 By morning
we'd counted fifty (species *Globicephala melaena*)
and Radio Ulster was construing a history. They'd left a sister
rotting on a Cornish beach, and then come here, to this dim
smoke-throated cistern, where the emptying tide leaves a scum
of musselshell and the smell of landfill and drains.
To mourn? Or to warn? Day drummed its thumbs
on their globular foreheads.

                 Neither due,
nor quarry, nor necessary, nor asked for, nor understood
upon arrival – what did we reckon to dress them in?
Nothing would fit. Not the man in oilskin working in the warehouse
of a whale, from the film of Sir Shackleton's blasted *Endeavour*,
as though a hill had opened onto fairytale measures
of blubber and baleen, and this was the money-
god's recompense;

                 not the huge Blue
seen from the sky, its own floating eco-system, furred
at the edges with surf; nor the unbridgeable flick
of its three-storey tail, bidding goodbye to this angular world
before barrelling under. We remembered a kind of singing,
or rather our take on it: some dismal chorus of want and wistfulness
resounding around the planet, alarmed and prophetic,
with all the foresight we lack –

                                                though not one of us
heard it from where we stood on the beaches and car-parks
and cycle-tracks skirting the water. What had they come for?
From Carrickfergus to Helen's Bay, birdwatchers with binoculars
held sway while the city sat empty. The whales grew frenzied.
Children sighed when they dived, then clapped as they rose
again, Christ-like and shining, from the sea, though they could have been
dying out there,

                                        smack bang
in the middle of the ferries' trajectory, for all we knew.
Or attempting to die. These were Newfoundland whales,
radically adrift from their feeding grounds, but we took them
as a gift: as if our own lost magnificent ship
had re-entered the Lough, transformed and triumphant,
to visit us. As if those runaway fires on the spines of the hills
had been somehow extinguished...

                                For now,
they were here. And there was nothing whatsoever to be said.
New islands in the water between Eden and Holywood.

Lullaby

When I can't sleep, you speak to me of trees.
Of the bald-eyed Eucalyptus
that flared in your back yard
like an astounded relative –
pointing to the honey bees in their rickety hives
your brother had abandoned.

Sometimes the tree was avuncular.
Arch with its secrets.
How it boasted, on days
your mother
hung sugarwater,
the delicate surgery of humming birds.

Contrail

Nightly now, insomnia lays its thumb
upon my forehead – an any how, Ash Wednesday cross.
Which, instead of insisting *Thou Shalt Pass*

to the Angel of Anxiety, hovering over the stairway,
beckons it in, at 3am, to unsettle me gently
with its insidious wings

Sometimes my mother and father.
Sometimes neither.
Sometimes childlessness, stretching out into the ether

like a plane

Little House in the Big Woods

Some things we shared.
Like the *Little House
in the Big Woods*, which for me
occurred prophetically

in the voice of Mrs Ledley
inside the free-milk sickish smell
of primary six. I remember
the enormity

of living in a hill;
leeches in the creek
and the slither of blood
they left in their wake

as a mark of trespass.
Our classroom windows
would be crying, as usual,
and out on the rim

of the playground,
crows' heads in rows
would be cocked to one
side, like policemen's.

But we were afloat
on an unstoppable continent:
each hand-built house
giving way to the next
                      as fast

as you could toss a hot potato
into glittering space
on a sleigh ride
after a syrup party…

For you it read differently –
the overdue library book
you couldn't give up.
As summer rolled on its back

and the driveway evaporated,
you would carry it out
past the sun-blistered gate
to your cubby-hole under the carport.

An apron of eggs.
Where your love for
the soon-to-be blinded sister
bloomed like a cold sore.
                              We swap

reminiscences we don't understand.
Squash (a word which was never
explained) in the rafters.
Pa's toleration of Indians.

Juist

They thought me too thin. I'd vomited all morning on the ship from Norddeich
and felt more fragile than I looked. At noon the sun cleared over the island –
clean as a coin where the water ended it, and held, whole, in the centre of vision
until proximity halved, then quartered it. Farms to the left without crops.
To the right, a sky of kites, kissing aggressively.

Nineteen. My first job. Time. And my life unavoidably occurring in stages
predictable from birth and regular as menstruation. The next station,
a landscape to change in. A resort in the North Sea for Germans
no one I knew had heard of, where one white side of the island was beach
and the other side, mud. Nine weeks to be stepped onto, crossed over, stepped off of.

The family fed me soup and a schnitzel and seemed disappointed.
Regular islandmen downed schnapps at the bar – pink, clear, frozen, on fire –
while the lies in my letter rose into the atmosphere and hung there:
the eight brothers and sisters I'd somehow invented to prove housework flair
and a willingness to share; German; French; Italian; Spanish.

When my first customer requested tap water, somewhere an executioner
cocked his gun and grinned. A word I'd never heard of. My notebook shook.
New tables terrified me with their limitless stores of unencountered vocabulary.
My face, rigid in panic as though the wind had changed, followed my body,
dislodged and desolate, for a week. To some I was merely bait;

others discovered a kindness in themselves they never knew existed
and enthused so warmly over unordered dishes I secretly wept.
The Captain (my own appellation) flung me like a tennis ball from table to table
and I bounced and skidded till closing time. He thought me a thief,
and at bedtime demanded a reckoning of coins as a pseudo-sadistic ritual.

I was exhausted, and then my body broke itself in.
A customer photographed me (*du als Kellnerin*) and I pinned the image
above my bed as a witness to the unthinkable. I became streamlined –
two plaits, soft shoes, trousers with pockets, a calculator, and across my heart
every salad, every stew, every fish, every meat dish on the menu, and every note and coin.

A kitchen help came from the East. A year since the GDR
had so spectacularly effaced itself, and he was here, saving money for six people.
One night he loomed over my bed, smashing imaginary plates against the wall.
Then he asked me to dance. By the time they gave me a door key my wages were missing.
He spent his last night alone in the dunes before vanishing.

The North Sea current was strong. Bathing times changed with the tides.
On afternoons off, I swam as far as the flags. Whatever way my shift fell,
I worked twelve hours, but I still always stole to the sea, even at midnight.
Once, after thunder, lightning was swimming in sea water, and waves, peeling
apart from themselves, hurled phosphorescent plankton into visual ecstasy…

And all this for me. I'd cycle three miles to the harbour –
no cars on the island, deliveries came by pony – and sit glued
as full moons bounced up over the water, glad to be lonely, and greedy
for the island skies unbroken by buildings and the island stars no streetlight
diminished or dimmed. Night skies on Juist were miraculous. My *aurora borealis.*

And stories of course. The semi-professional corpse-hunter who trawled
fifteen miles of beach every morning scouring for a reward:
the over-confident, the victims of heart-attack, the drowned washed back
to where they started. A birth on the restaurant floor.
The year the sea between Juist and Norddeich froze.

I bought every newspaper the morning the Gorbachev coup broke on the world.
Once, in the middle of a do-able dinner shift, I started to cry, the first time
the Captain had seen me. He gave me a strawberry schnapps and patted my head.
Grown men have cried here, we thought you'd cry sooner.
I washed all my own clothes in the sink till my knuckles bled.

I discovered a derelict hotel. The Nazis built it big to match
their enormous year of 1936: a challenge to the horizon. Now gone to ruin
and seabird colonies. Only the basement stayed open as a bar.
I slammed vodka bananas on my second last night there
and lost reason on the dance floor. My one night off of the summer.

And then leaving threatened. My self grown raw and tremulous and impressionable
in the space between changing shape, and then to be torn from the source
of everything painful, everything valuable. I cycled the island,
willing the skies and sands to monopolise vision –
not to let me leave without them. The morning the ship sailed

breakfast was Christmas, with cards and gifts and forgiveness,
and Juist grew initially wider, my back to the sea.
I carried my grief on my knees, spread out like a hanky. The island was emptying.
Islanders were shutting up shop, banking the profits of summer, imagining darkness –
long nights in which no work would be necessary – and
the coming of frost.

China

1

Tack up a screen before dawn and ready the inks.
There is a country which does not exist and which must be shown.
Steady the ingredients.

2

A tunnel of trees. My brother and I on the top
of an empty double-decker in Derbyshire.
The absence-from-home of summer
becoming a scab to be picked over. The bus pulled up

by a pub, as the greenery scratching
at the window ended and we were given a field
with a horse and a dog and a red child
in it, waving.

Sunlight was there like a wall
and halved everything. In my head I was singing
This is Happening This is Happening This is Happening.
A boy bounced his way down the aisle

and started smoking, when time
opened. Or stopped. Or almost stalled
and the boy and my brother and the bus and the world
disappeared on the prick of a needle – pop! – and I

sat sideways avoiding the gap.
And then I saw I was enormous
and in another kind of tunnel. That I was lost.
That there was no going back.

3

Conjure the Yangtze and the Yellow River
And bring them a matter of hours together
On the same train line and both of them seen
Through semi-darkness on a flickering screen
Which is and is not a window. Blow
Over the waters to buckle them. Add snow.

4

The King of the Sea
is awash with vainglory
in Beijing.

He has caused havoc
with his aquatic
animals. Now

he wants to clobber
the Monkey King
(the destined-to-win

Monkey King)
who is wagging his tongue
for some rust-free weapons

from the Sea King's
underwater arsenal.
The Sea King's antennae

are aquiver
with put-upon-
power. The Monkey King,

in his ecstatic
clothing, is too yellow
to be trusted.

The Sea King's refusal
amuses him.
He is fluid

as a cartoon and brimful
with trickery.
He does not know

how colour
is protected.
In a square

given over
to the Palace Executioner
the cobblestones

are mimicking the sun.
For coming too close
to the Only One –

See the desiccated yellows
of the colour convicts
flutter and flare.

5

Evening. Beijing. And farewell to Mao's mausoleum
through the glass, ablaze in the nerves of the Square of Heaven
like everlasting Christmas. The bus forces us on:
another station, another train, another city, another season.
Advertising flickers in the waiting room. That night I dive like a child –
borne aloft by the train's engine, or like one born again in its mild
motion, the shunt and click of the carriages over the sidings
the soporific tenderness of a language I do not recognise –
and re-surface at nine, an hour beyond breakfast time.
The mine wheels, factories, fish farms, and allotments
battling for space between slack-blackened tenements
have receded now into the north. Here the sky is unfolding the blue
cloth of itself on a new country, or on a country which never grew
old to begin with. Spinach, pak choi, cabbage greens, lettuce,
geese sunning themselves among shiny brown cowls of the lotus

and an echo-less emptiness, a sense of perspective too wide
and too high for the eye to take in. Two crows collide
in a rice field, then are flung backwards out of their war
as the train pushes on. We loiter like Oliver in the dining car.
Brunch comes as simmering bowls of noodles, under a film
of oil, and we sit watching the landscape unfurl like a newsreel
into history. By noon, foothills are banking to the south.
By two, we're approaching a network of tunnels blasted out
of the Xi'an Qin Mountains. Blackness falls clean as a guillotine
on the children in pairs by the trackside, and then again
on the man and his son who will walk all afternoon into evening
before they are home. We enter Sichuan without rupturing
any visible line of division, though dinner at five is brimming with chillies:
dried and diced and fried with the seeds inside, while the extraordinary
Sichuan pepper balloons into flavour under our tongues. And all along
darkness is gathering itself in. I see a boy and a woman
lit up by the flare of a crop fire, but can no longer believe in them.
Windows have turned into mirrors the length of the train.
Hours pass, and there is only my white face, strained
in its hopelessness, my failure to catch the day in my hands like a fish
and have it always. The train descends from the soil terraces.
Electricity switches the world back on: town after coal-dusted town
streams by in the rain, revealing its backdoor self, its backyard frown,
until all converge in a dayglo glare at the end of the line and we merge
with our destination. We have been dropped to the bottom of somewhere
blurred and industrial, where the yellow of the Yangtze meets the green
of its tributary, the city with a name like the din of a smithy: Chongqing.

6

All night the hammers broke the dark
But then the dark went on
I rose and pulled the curtains back
A semaphore of cranes

Gesticulating deftly
To each other, to the sky
A city in conspiracy
To keep the sun at bay

25

And in the fog I could not tell
What was falling down
From what was rising up again
Both wore a hanging chain

And both were eye-less, light-less, stalled
Both held their form elsewhere
The past or future part-way entered
Into this wounded sphere

I left the hold of our hotel
To walk along the river
Across from me, a chargrilled hill
Of building like a fever

And junks that could not carry
The weight of what they bore
Dying in a tributary
Inches from the shore

The sky had almost lightened
To midday's faint resolve
When a mother tugging a wayward child
Brushed against my sleeve

And brought me through a quarter
Of rubble-matted streets
Where a woman washing her waist-length hair
Stood wringing it like a sheet

And stopped me at a doorway
And pointed down its throat
I photographed it dumbly
Lost to what it meant

Her urgency diminished
I smiled I had to go
The air was thick between us
With all I could not know

Day gave without a whimper
I found myself re-caged
Staring through the filter
Of money's privilege

I find I have made a ghost
of you – I'm sorry – as I
aimed my camera foolishly
at the passing coloratura
of mountains and fields,
and snapped them anyway,
knowing I'd never get them back
the way they were being given,
at that precise instant, and caught them,
yes alright, adequately enough, but somehow
also caught your watchful face
filling the window without
its source. Confucius refuses
to speak about spirits. *Till you know*
about the living, how are you
to know about the dead? he pronounces
to the ever-curious Tzu-lu.
And I wonder, if I can make ghosts
of the living with my dinky, digital
machine, is it possible I can also
make the dead visible? And I set my camera
more deliberately now on the vast, peopleless
expanse, then check its screen
to see if I've got anything
in its wide-eyed little net.
I don't know what I expected –
one or two of the million Yangtze
drowned, perhaps, still draining their ears
by banging the sides of their heads, or looking after
the vanishing tumult of the train
for directions home?

Ever been washed
by a crowd? My mother dragging me
to the cold water tap and
jamming my finger under it
the day I brushed it across

the cooker-top to see
if it was on, *to numb it*,
she said, but it wasn't
like that
at all. It was

winter, we were
baking in the kitchen and
I could still smell a scrap
of skin frying in the back-
ground when the cold

hit home – prodding
the length of my arm in a surge
of pain, an ironic
remedy of extremes.
And it was oddly

uplifting to be suspended
there with your body peeled
back to the nerve all
over again in a matter
of seconds, so disarmingly

alive. In four train stations within
fourteen days I turned my head
to a conundrum. After a night
and a day and a night of being carried
along in a capsule –

a bed, a quilt, a pillow, a night-
light, a table, tea, a window, a
radio – I'd uncurl onto
the platform, grey and
exhausted, as though I'd walked

the hours that divided us
from our origin. We were alone
the whole time, moving like
automatons from compartment to
dining car, then back

again, with only the fruit-
man to disturb our corridor
with his casual calling. The train's nose
under the station awning would steam
with exertion; we'd be cracking

our wrists, or avoiding
the press, or yawning, and then,
imperceptibly, finally noticing
the river of people disgorged from a mile
of doors and flooding towards

the exit sign. There must have been
thousands of them, our shadow-
travellers, and we'd been marooned
in the midst of them. They'd have sat
upright all day and

all night on benches as hard
as amazonite, pressed five
to a row and room somehow for
rice pots and rucksacks and armfuls
of jackets, flasks,

blankets. Thirty hours
at a stretch and seeming as fresh
as if they'd just stepped out
of a ten-hour sleep
on a cloud –

and with somewhere to get to
fast: time to stare back
at me the way I was staring
at them, an extravagance.
I stayed to one side, watching

them flow like an out-
going tide into the maw of each
city, and saw myself
caught in the pulse of their
striding, my greenish skin hurled

under water and hammering *I am*
here you are real this
is happening it is
redeemable – as though touching
them might be possible.

9

One day, China met China in the marketplace.
'How are you, China?' asked China, 'we haven't talked in so long.'
China answered: 'The things we have to say to one another,
        laid end to end, and side to side,
would connect the Great Wall with the Three Gorges Valley
        and stretch nine miles up towards the sun.'
'It's true,' replied China. 'We have a lot to catch up on.'

The Gobi from Air

1

Auden's face in age
looked like this place.

The same wind–chiselled flair.
The same doubt as to where

decorousness
really ought to begin and end.

Ten thousand barrels of sand
overturned

on the streets of Beijing in a year.
Some days they fear

that the earth
is raining.

2

His addiction to war
delivered him here –

a three-month-old letter
wherever he went.

His trains all avoided the front.
The Japanese shielded their eyes

from the sun, and kept on killing.
He toured warehouses, brothels, remembering,

out of everything,
damp fungus frothing

on the fingertips
of the mill girls in Shanghai.

Polar

after Brecht

My darling, lest you vanish back
To the vast frontier you fled from
Once its darkness
Failed to break –
Baying for bathwater, bedlinen, *me* –
Without a further word,
Allow these gifts:

Six pairs of pearl–stitch knitted socks,
An Aran with a fingered ridge, a scarf
To trap a boulder in.
For even though you're lean
And craven, I'd rather have you
Round and down and rollable.
I want to hap you up

So that you stagger off, surrounded
By my warmth, on your journey
North. I want to wrap
Your delectable backside
(Which I chew on so immoderately
When I'm out of my right mind)
In all the wool of Scotland.

Forgive me this redress. Forgive
The need to staunch my loneliness
On your enormous absence.
Even the furniture sags without you.
I invent a war to send you
Off to, but it's only a war
With nature. They say it's winter

When you're up there
Nine months of the year
(The solstice dragging its feet
With the weight of the planet);
That the sky is merely on fire
With its own futility; and the snow geese –
Inconsequential company.

On Omitting the Word 'Just' from my Vocabulary

And here I am in a room I don't recognise, being
angular and contemporary, with its own
unabashed light source and the table clear.

I must be somewhere Scandinavian.
Where weather is decisively one way
or the other, and summer,

or winter, will not brook contradiction.
Even the ornaments (such as they are)
are purposeful: a stone dog stares into the fireplace

as though pitting itself against fire
for the next quarter-century.
(How you cannot say 'just' and 'pregnancy'.)

There is a fissure in store for me here.
There are no wall hangings. Or rugs.
The door is locked against me.

My own audacity in coming here
astounds me. Yet I step purposefully.
I swell uncontrollably.

Beyond in the hallway
the tongue of a bell is banging against its shell.
It sounds like a coffin lid,

or as definitive.
It is marking the hours until I break into two
and lose/gain everything.

Advice

You think it ugly: drawing lines with a knife
Down the backs of those writers we exist to dislike. But it's life.

One is disadvantaged by illustrious company
Left somehow undivided. Divide it with animosity.

Don't be proud –
Viciousness in poetry isn't frowned on, it's *allowed.*

Big fish in a big sea shrink proportionately.
Stake out your territory

With stone walls, steamrollers, venomous spit
From the throat of a luminous nightflower. Gerrymander it.

Reading the Greats

Is it for their failures that I love them?
Ignoring the regulation of *Selected Poems*,
with everything in that should be in –
all belted & buttoned & shining –
I opt instead for omnivorous *Completes*.
For their froth. Their spite. For avoidable mistakes:
Larkin on Empire, say, or Plath on Aunts.

The thrill of when they dip, trip up, run out
of things to write about before they start,
is the consolation of watching
a seascape suddenly drained and stinking
of flies & fishheads & bladderwrack.
And the tide impossibly distant. And no way back.
Yes, I love them for that.

In Praise of Salt

I'm salting an egg in the morning.
It's one year on. The radio is documenting
the threats we face… The cut and lash
of voices pitched to shatter glass.

For a second I don't hear the kettle boil
and wonder: if Iraq mined salt instead of oil?
At Leonardo's table, salvation spilled
as Judas scattered salt. And we're still poised to kill.

In India they made salt and shook an Empire.
Salt makes us what we are, and takes us there.

The Wound Man

for Federico García Lorca

It would have been a kind of action replay,
only worse. The white handkerchiefs.
The unimaginable collapse. The day
the markets crashed and unleashed
unknowing through the New York streets

saw you transfixed, a witness in Times Square,
as the world went down in hysterical laughter
and diminishing shrieks. Then thudded over.
All hope in the gutter, blooded and lost. How you loathed
the reflections of clouds in the skyscrapers

and the glittering rings of the suicides.
It was all one in New York: the manacled roses, oil on the Hudson,
financial devastation. Had you survived,
Federico, say, Franco's henchmen,
or the war that was to open like a demon from his person,

or the later war, and all the intervening years
between that fall of faith and this, what would you think?
Would you know what has happened here,
the way we do not know what has happened? Where
would your fury go? We shiver on the brink

of an ending, and a war stretches in front of us,
we stand where you stood. As for me,
I see the Wound Man walking, tall and imperious,
through the streets of America, surly
and muscular, from the textbook of Paracelsus.

He's been badly hit. There are weapons through every part of him.
A knife in the cheek; an arrow in the thigh;
someone has severed his wrist bones, on a whim,
and thrust a sword into his eye.
They've flung razors at his flesh to pass the time.

And yet he rears. Sturdy and impossible. Strong.
Loose in the world. And out of proportion.

Clocks

The sadness of their house is hard to defeat. There are at least three clocks per room.
There are two people with nothing to do but to be in each room and be separate.
The person each room was decorated by was seconded to a plot in a cemetery
that is walked to every day, and tended like a bedroom sanctuary. No notice given.
The clocks do all the talking. He visits the grave in the middle of a three-hour loop
and knows the year of completion of every castle in Ireland. His route
is always the same: the round tower via the aqueduct via the cemetery via the ramparts
via the Battle of Antrim during the Rising of the United Irishmen in 1798,
the slaughter of which is more present if he's deep in the morning
of his April wedding breakfast or locked into the moment they fitted the oxygen mask
and she rolled her bruised eyes back. She is unable to find the stop for the bus to Belfast
and stays indoors. The nets turn the daylight white and empty.
She has worn the married life of her sister so tightly
over her own, the noise of the clocks makes her feel almost without skin.
Sometimes she sits in her sister's chair, and feels guilty.
She has *Countdown* for company and a selective memory –
the argument at the funeral with her niece over jewellery and, years ago,
the conspiracy to keep her single, its success. Time settles over each afternoon
like an enormous wing, when the flurry of lunchtime has left them
and the plates have already been set for tea. He reads extensively –
from *Hitler and Stalin, Parallel Lives*, to *Why Ireland Starved* –
but has taken to giving books away recently to anyone who calls.
Winter or summer, evenings end early: they retire to their separate rooms
at least two hours before sleep. It falls like an act of mercy
when the twenty-two clocks chime eight o'clock in almost perfect unison.

Aunt Sarah's Cupboards and Drawers

Are a job she doesn't feel up to anymore.
She sits in her high-backed chair watching television
as dust falls over the soup-tin lids
in the tin cupboard in the kitchen.

Last year she followed the sun's eclipse
by the day's collapsing wattage in her sitting-room,
cheerful with photos of relatives' children.
She said she watched as it shuttered each face in unison

and then released them. When she broke her hip
she remembers something picking her up and then dropping
her on it – *like cracking an egg* –
and that the picking-up part was a cradling.

She always looks for Venus
and tells me more about the moon than I can write down.
She weighs the hazards of waiting too long at a bus-stop
carefully on each palm

before going to town. Her life
was wider than this once – choir practice, Butlin's,
walks to the neighbouring village in summer without thinking
twice about it – but never by much.

Absences Also

Take shape,　　　　　　　take sup. See
our lives seep up　　　　　with missing children
like awareness of the dead　among the overly sensitive.

Icarus

To give forever of oneself because oneself, though puckered
and sagged, has not yet been torn and has air in its silks still.

To swing over the river to enter this life and exit this life
buoyant. Or at least, however precariously, aloft. With muscle.

Not to fall to where they have fallen and from where they can never cross.
Such faces.

I stayed up for years. Disregarding their expressions.
Their mud-stranded resignation. In tributaries.

And then my son.
And what he did to boys.

Forgiveness

Comes afterwards. Like a nurse with a tea tray and a sleeping pill.

Relies on two. No more, no less. Is indivisible.

It cannot be willed, just welcomed. Immune to duty.

Is desired and disbelieved in equally, like a menopausal pregnancy.

(Last night I dreamt a cancer of the retina and a simultaneous cancer of the bowel.

I'd been shitting blood for months. The eye was inoperable.

And there we were, kicking our heels off a house wall under a window sill.

It was summer, suddenly, predictably. We were both restful.

I'm dying, I said, as a pain subsided. You put on sunglasses.)

I hope that sooner or later, this side of the divide, or afterwards, it happens.

Driving Alone on a Snowy Evening

after Frost

There is no reason that I know
To go on waking, eating, so
I turn the urgent wipers off
And watch the screen sift up with snow.

They'll conjure emptiness, despair,
Disease in the wings, a failed career.
Those inward, ticking moments when
The seduction of stopping obliterates fear.

The car purrs on. I do not brake.
The choice of crash I leave to fate.
A tree, a bridge, a railway line.
Behind the brightness dark shapes wait.

The snow and ceiling kiss, then meet.
The view's as white as a winding sheet.
The heart still beats *repeat repeat.*
The heart still beats *repeat repeat.*

Migraine

It wasn't long before my vision blurred.
The shock. The chocolate. The thirst.
Eight hours in. The leader's face went slack
from the left side, as though his cheekbone cracked
and slithered free of him, weeping gunshot.
Then a tangle of darkness like a Rorschach blot
where his expression had been, opening inward...
I knew what it was once the starlight started.
Not liberation – no special forces falling from the ceiling.
This was my cross, my cleansing,
my monthly reckoning,
my migraine time rolled round
again, to take me over and close me down.
The piled explosives by the fifteenth aisle
looked eaten with flame, but shimmeringly so, while
dying fires pulsed off and on along the stage
as though the threads of things had frayed
to let the light through. My awful light. Light in the wrong place.
Like the sun at midnight or blood on the moon's face.
Eleven when it first descended. Had I gone blind
to see the whole world punctured from behind?
Pain was payment afterwards. It fell in blows –
planes hitting runways, slapstick pianos
crashing down stairs or hurtling out of windows.
I learned to turn to the wall. To strain to be empty.
To be animal and insular in sickness. To ossify.
To reckon blessings on my fingers as I wept.
The half who were women were padded and desperate.
Their voices were slick with contempt for the hostages
and lust for an ending that would splatter their message
from the newsstands of Moscow to the gun slums of Washington.
Their faces were veiled in black. Their hurt souls shone.
There is a war, they said, *somewhere off the map from where you are,*
and we will bring it to you. Horror poured out in a glittering theatre,
and held there. Act II. They stormed the stage yelling
Allahu Akbar. And now I was blinded by lightning
while my head was filling with blood like a black pudding.
I came for the stage effects: the bomber
from the war of my grandfather
falling out of the sky. The revolution glimpsed through fire and ash.

The love interest. Songs to sing in the bath,
afterwards. We were fed confectionary from the interval kiosk
which made my body bloom. Water was scarce.
Talk was policed.
Russia's first musical had its throat sliced.

The Yellow Emperor's Classic

after Gong Sun

The body is China.
Middle Kingdom between here
and hereafter, it is compromised from the start.
Messengers are important.

China has been an imperial system
for centuries, and repeats itself endlessly.
The heart is its Emperor.
All other organs are the Emperor's courtiers –

see poor pericardium
go slack with deflected shame.
A king may never be blamed directly, so
heart-sac swallows heart-blows uncomplainingly.

We are constantly at the mercy
of pernicious influences: cold, damp, dry, wind,
heat and summer heat. (There are two kinds
of summer in the Chinese calendar.)

These are also known as the six evils.
When the spirit exits, it exits
from the back of the neck. The body
opens and shuts itself to damage

like a gate refusing to be latched.
We muster control
of our orifices.
We fight back.

Sexual energy resides in the kidney,
lowest of all yin organs
and root of the body tree.
Desire is pre-heaven essence.

It flows before birth,
bestowed wherever our souls
are stowed, in a limited vial
and fatally expendable.

There is a highway
of sexual awakening,
a road rather than a river
in spite of water.

At puberty a dignitary
(from heaven, ultimately)
slashes with his sword the blood-
silk ribbon and cries 'Open!'

Old Liver General
must ensure all *qi* troops
now pass
in an orderly fashion.

For there must be sex. True, too much
depletes our pre-heaven essence
and can result in weaknesses
of the lower trunk. But too little is catastrophic.

Like trying to survive
without our opposite
inside us
when opposites equal life.

China is haunted by celibate women
at risk from surfeit of yin. Listen.
Withering from within, they are homesick
and wandering. Vengeful as ghosts.

Zero

for Joseph

Whatever else it was he stole from the East –
indigo, gold, a brace of abused and temporary women,
frankincense, the inevitable spice or two,
or the fruit that shed itself with such feral sweetness
on the tongue it begged re-naming –
Alexander also stowed nothing –
that double nick in the Babylonian plaque which,
of everything, was the easiest to store
(the women were a nightmare)
precisely because it lived nowhere
and therefore everywhere: in two spare horseshoes
angled together, in the kiss of a thumb and forefinger,
in the sigh at the bottom of a poured-out water jar,
in the memory of some noon-white city square
wherever luck ran out, or faith, or anger –

                                                                    but

when Alexander delivered zero to the Greeks
they turned and saw (or thought they saw)
a wellhead blacken in front of them –
an incredulous, bricked-in 'O' –
unravelling into inkiness like a sleeve, the kind
you might toss a stone into and never hear the splash,
though you stand and wait, your ear awash in silence,
for an hour – and over it the bric-a-brac of kitchens appeared
suspended in the sunshine – knives, lemons, sieves, pots, bowls –
a funnel of dailyness, which the wellhead then swallowed
like a child, and, sensing where it could lead,
this number/no-number that would eat the world,
the Greeks turned back to Alexander in the advancing shade
and smiled: for there were still angles, there were still
three old angels skipping over heaven carrying harps and signs.

Stepfather

When Cathy came to New Zealand, my stepfather Charles
put on his woollen vest and Swan overcoat and peaked cap
with a rainbow embroidered on it and took us to see the waterfall.

He was a bushman: had grown up in the bush Up North
before ever there was a town the way Whangarei is a town today
with its flat whites and yellow taxicabs and Maori women drivers. Yes,

had shouldered his way into adulthood, into being army-wed,
from the bed of an eel-breeding creek, on the back of a Kauri trunk,
against the hard flat palm of a forest that – decades afterwards –

had still not been felled. So he knew where to take us and how to take us,
that winter afternoon, in the handclapping rain of the Waitakeres,
donning that pack of his as though he were back in Vietnam,

where all his booming dreams still happen, his casual jockey saunter
a bowsprit through the leaves, though he knew exactly what we might find
and wasn't daunted. And yet how tenderly they would park their cars –

some even bothering to hood the steering wheel in chains –
in viewing spots anywhere along the Scenic Drive, before breaking off
into the trees, when he would get the call to go and find them.

He'd cut them down after days sometimes. The branches of Pongas
unfisted beside the railway line and the birds were indefatigable.
The rain was bringing the dark on early but you could still see

the entire steaming basin of greenery swallowing water
on your left side (my mother in her innocence asking,
the day she arrived from Ireland, *but who planted all this?*)

and Cathy and Joseph and Charles and I were increasingly more like
forked poles in a river than people as we came up to the mouth
of the train tunnel and waded inside. He could woo wood pigeons

just by talking to them and once one had rested on his hand.
Away from the thwack and clatter of the downpour and where
entrance and exit were two equidistant reminders of daylight

lived the glow-worms he spoke of, that were not worms at all
but a little boy's peel-and-stick galaxy, a lace of green needlepoint,
winking on after lights-out over the bunk bed. Out at the other end

and evening was gathering pace in the forest far faster than we'd predicted,
returning each towering layer of flax to one vast, dripping canopy.
By the rudiments of a siding shed – a rejected Korean asylum seeker

had survived here for a fortnight on trapped possums and stream water –
we angled ourselves for the climb and veered right, up through the breathing
trees, and what dusk there was had swung shut on a solitariness

of moss and lichen and spider orchids. Charles cut the way out in front of us
without slowing, insisting we still had time, his mind – who knows –
on the nights he'd lain down on the floor of a Singapore jungle,

with only a net to shelter in, and the insects in the air had shrieked
so accusingly at every rigid angle of his body, he couldn't sleep.
It had been raining now for a week. The Waitakere Dam was full –

even from here we could hear it batter itself over the brim
and the waterfall was the same: choked and slick and incandescent
in the dim cave it had made for itself. Our breaths came hard

and alien in the clearing as we took its kiss on our skin.
Charles stood like a conquistador, hand on one hip, looking up.
But already I was imagining the journey back, down through the slithering

dark, all three of us steady in his flashlight's wake, hitting the railway track
and then on through the tunnel and then up to the steps by the concrete expanse
of the dam face, and into the house near the watercress bank where my life

had been riveted for months. Our homecoming chorus the hunger
of owls, fierce and unassuageable – *morpork! morpork!* –
and Charles cocking his head at the sound of them as though they could speak.

The State of the Prisons

A History of John Howard, Prison Reformer, 1726–1790

As for me, I will behold thy face in righteousness:
I shall be satisfied when I awake, with thy likeness.
                                        Psalm 17:15

I am a stranger and a pilgrim here.
I burn my letters, decline a monument, take heart
From the body's incontinence. The spirit departs.
The field hospitals of Russia with their horrendous dead
Must carry me home to the Lord my Maker
Where all my fathers' fathers stand assembled.

I see these soldiers' faces when I sleep.
And then they cloud and clear again as the child's
Who stopped me on the road to ask the time
And tried to steal my watch. How sick she is.
And then she splits, becomes three women beating hemp
In a bridewell, missing eyelids…

Death has no terrors for me.
I have ridden the Devil's coach road, I have discovered
It leads, in every city in Europe, to the mansions of governors.
Powders fizz in a glass. The admiral who has travelled
Thirty miles to smile encouragingly
Tries to change the subject but his voice unravels.

Death sits in my frame. And death shall have dominion
Where all bodies are. 70,000 Russian soldiers died the year before
I washed up on the far shore of the Crimea.
This figure summoned me to Stepanovka –
A detour from my quest to find the origin
Of plague. Now all such quests are over.

There is a village where a river flows
Through a grove of pine tree. It is peaceful and obscure,
Called Dauphigny. A Frenchman I befriended came from there.
We passed it on our journey south.
Bury me here in my chapel clothes
And let my body face the river mouth.

Fame saddens heaven. Suffer no stone to be raised to me,
Nor details of my life and works be given at the gravebed,
Nor mourners come. Erect a sundial over my head
Instead of an inscription. Read from the psalms
Of beholding His face in righteousness. Forget me. To posterity,
I leave a syphilitic son, and a vision of prisons.

God sent an earthquake when I was twenty-nine
And lured my soul to suffering like moths to the flame.
November 1755. As my first wife was lain
In an oak box in Whitechapel, 20,000 attested dead
Flared across the pages of the *Gentleman's Magazine*.
The death toll left me breathless, but decided.

Resolved for Portugal, I dismissed my servants,
Sorted my affairs, and was heading for the wreckage on the Lisbon Packet
On the 14th day in January, when the French attacked.
We were captured as prisoners of war, whipped,
And forced on our knees to swear a blood-felt testament
To dungeon existence. Later we were shipped

To Carhaix, then finally released. I came home.
Washed. Grew well. In time became Sheriff of Bedford.
The villagers and tenants prospered.
My French adventure faded from view. And then the County Trials,
Irregular as women, rolled round again to Cardington,
And everything changed. At the first sitting of the Assizes

The prisoners entered, pulling on long chains.
A muscle jerked in my thumb. The judge was eminent,
Bored, ecclesiastical, inured to the stench of sweat and excrement
That flowered where they stood. I was reeling back to a stone hole
And darkness interminable, as the felons' crimes
Were pronounced against them in a nasaloid drone.

When it was over, I barked six questions at the Crown officials.
Why are they not clean? Why so thin?
Why ill? Why are felons and debtors, women and men,
Chained and tried together? Why, when chosen for release,
Do debtors stay listed on the turnkey's roll call?
What fees remain to pay? Justice sat asleep

In a rolled wig. I metamorphosed into an enthusiast.
And so it was my journey started to every prison in Europe,
Shuttling between nations like an evangelist. Or *a Cook
Of the Unfortunate* (as Burke put it). I, too, was on a voyage of discovery.
I, too, would make maps. A continent of misery, unchartered, vast,
Opened before my eyes. I vowed to regulate the colony.

Lord, keep me solitary to do Thy will.
My second wife, delivered of our only son
In 1765, afterwards died of a womb infection.
I was not designed for intimacy. The boy bothered me,
Mooning in my shadow like a criminal,
And sickly. I tried Lockean discipline: cold baths, daily;

Wet socks; no sweetmeats. He promised to obey me,
Even irrationally. I sat him in the root house once in February
And didn't lock the door, to see if he would stay
Despite the cold. (He stayed.) He was sent away to school, and manhood,
When he was four years old. Unshackled, free,
At lodgings in the capital, I joined the Kingdom of the Wicked.

Ah London! Thou vast ship of distress!
With Newgate at thy helm, ferrying the damned to Tyburn.
How many more were cut down by contagion?
The turnkey looked astounded when I asked to descend
To the felons' wards, armed with a notebook, and an all-but-useless
Phial of vinegar. Gaol fever, the pox, the flux, the pestilence

Raged down there. Later they claimed I was cloaked in righteousness –
I ascribe my immunity to God's Purpose and shallow breathing.
Even after riots in 1780 left Old Newgate smouldering,
They rebuilt the bastion with its heart intact.
I see it as I first entered it: putrid with grime, lice
Crunching underfoot, prostitutes parading in their Sunday hats.

I extended my research, living mostly on the road,
Eating and sleeping between prisons. My carriage stank
Obnoxiously in summer, so I switched to horseback.
Ipswich has no fireplace, Ely no straw, in Durham six prisoners
Were chained to the floor of a dungeon under a courtyard,
Up to their ankles in sewer water.

Like Luther, I made a list of grievances.
They say in hell the damned are separated, each to their own offence.
I saw both sexes sprawl like dogs in the marketplace
Through most of the prisons in England, the debtor drink gin with the highwayman,
The youthful and the innocent confined without allowances
For innocence or youth. I steadied myself for a reformation.

4

They said I rode like a horseman of the Apocalypse.
My circuit broadened: to Scotland, to Ireland, to the Continent.
It intensified: I saw schools, workhouses, hospitals for the indigent,
Asylums for the insane. I saw those confined by quarantine
As well as by crime. In truth, each journey was slow and treacherous:
60,000 miles of stony road, potholes, ditches and slime

Stretch between Dublin and Constantinople. And I remember them all.
I was travelling now obsessively.
The boy spent school holidays at Cardington without me.
My servant sent reports. *There are problems, Sir,*
Wrote Thomasson, warily, almost daring to be vocal,
Problems of a certain delicate nature – . Ignorance was my error.

Fame was busy, ever preceding me. I was never alone
For long in a new city. Popes and princesses asked me to dine.
When Catherine the Great demanded my company, I declined
On account of her lax morality. I thought her a glorified courtesan.
Joseph of Austria was a true compatriot: not a month on the throne
And he'd visited every prison and hospital, sometimes with only a footman.

I was summoned by the Roman Fisherman. He was non-committal.
I know you Englishmen do not value these things,
But the blessing of an old man can do you no harm. I kissed his rings.
Then ignoring decorum, inspired by the Lord,
I mentioned my time with the Inquisitor General
Of Valladolid of Spain. He was gravely discomforted.

Shall my tongue be tied from speaking the truth
By any earthly king? To term that court, by an ingenious ruse,
the HOLY Inquisition, was a monstrous abuse.
I saw its instruments: Scavenger's Daughter, Little Ease.
I took tea in a room with a garrulous oil painting, smooth
As sin, of 97 heretics on fire in a procession. Even the breeze

Was painted as a victory. And this was what had to stop.
This table wrapped in black cloth with a bible on it
Used to draw blood. This braying intolerance.
Power in the clotting of candle wax and confessions at midnight.
The Osnabrück Torture. The Terror of insignias. Pomp.
This being underground. We had to let in the light.

A lone voice in the wilderness? Perhaps.
But I wasn't a desert prophet. I didn't spin a vision out of nothing,
not attempt the Celestial City without researching everything.
I looked where long centuries had averted their gaze.
I made the commonest filth – the swarming of dungeon rats –
A suppurate state malaise.

My plan was simple, practical, and above all, cheap.
Salary the turnkeys. No profits to be gleaned from pimping,
Turning barman, extortion, or doctoring
In ignorance and at extravagant expense. No fees
For removing leg irons, access to the fireplace, or supplying cheese and meat.
No garnish to be sought off new arrivals. No hierarchies.

If idleness breeds vice, industry brings a smiling account balance
And the promise of self-sufficiency. Attach a factory,
A cloth works or a smelting house, to every penitentiary.
Let every inmate be supervised there. Out of such labour,
An income for provisions, heating, clothing and medicine, in accordance
With daily needs. Allow extra for good behaviour.

I came home famous. *The State of the Prisons* such a manifest success
It engendered an Act of Parliament. Yet all along,
Sickness was festering in my only son like sedition in a nation
With a missing king. The French Revolution unfurled across the Channel
As the desperate hints of scandalised servants converged into flesh
And betrayal. The boy was irrecoverable.

What example had I inculcated by wallowing in evil?
My absence gave licence to the deviant Thomasson,
Who defiled himself with numberless men, at dockside brothels in London,
Taking his charge along with him.
The boy contracted venereal disease, ravaged by the Devil
In a butler's turncoat. Syphilis had already attacked my son's facial skin

By the time I finally encountered him, flailing and spitting in my hallway.
Demented with hatred. Pretence was useless, sophistry over,
As he raved he had known neither father nor mother,
That I had twisted him with neglect. I wept. He was destined for an asylum.
Must reform cost exponentially? My conscience sears me, as with David I say:
O my son Absalom, my son, my son.

To ten poor families, who for ten long years
Have refused to visit an alehouse, five pounds.
Let us look to the regeneration of souls.
Assign every prison a chapel, and a chaplain.
Those who swing from the scaffold to inculcate fear
Are not only lost to Christ, they are lost to the Nation –

To its mines, and battlefields. *To ten more families,*
Not receiving parish funds, most constant
At church attendance, five pounds. Watch
All inmates ceaselessly. Ensure that the sexes are segregated,
And that prisoners are confined in sexual purity
By sleeping on their own. Let even their dreams be inspected.

To twenty poor widows, two guineas.
Let time be spent thinking of trespass.
Of what went wrong. And why. Teach them to ask forgiveness
So they can emerge from solitude like butterflies from a chrysalis.
Lead them to the wall of self-discovery
Which they will bleed upon, before they see their faces

Shining back at them. *One hundred pounds for the poorest prisoners*
Throughout the county gaols. No more haemorrhaging
The poor to Australia. No more rotting
On hulks along the Thames, as though this were the answer.
The people can be reclaimed, with ardour,
To their rightful inheritance. Making order stronger.

Five hundred pounds to a new society
For alleviating the miseries of public prisons
After my time is done. I have burned a single instance
Of concern, I do not trust Parliament as keepers of the flame
When I have vanished into heaven. Found a reform league to defy
Their wisdom. Mark it with my name.

My son to have whatever remains.
So much that I have left undone. And so much harm.
I shut out his invective, and instead return
To the obedient child, who stayed on until four, when darkness fell.
His frozen, painful hands were raw for days.
I kiss them well.

Notes

Flight
I am indebted here to Michael McKeon's *The Origins of the English Novel 1600–1740* (Baltimore, London: Johns Hopkins University Press, 1987), which first brought the 'miraculous' flight of Charles II in 1651 to my attention. Other details in the poem are taken from Samuel Pepys's *His Majesty Preserved: An Account of King Charles II's Escape after the Battle of Worcester,* first published in 1680 (London: Falcon Press, 1954).

The State of the Prisons
Two biographies of John Howard were crucial to the writing of this poem: Leona Baumgartner's *John Howard: Hospital and Prison Reformer* (Baltimore: Johns Hopkins University Press, 1939); and Martin Southwood's *John Howard: Prison Reformer* (London: Independent Press, 1958). The title of the poem comes from Howard's own publication, *The State of the Prisons,* first published in 1777.